**Editor**
Gabriel Arquilevich, M.A.

**Editorial Project Manager**
Ina Massler Levin, M.A.

**Editor in Chief**
Sharon Coan, M.S. Ed.

**Illustrator**
Howard Chaney

**Cover Artist**
Sue Fullam

**Art Coordinator**
Denice Adorno

**Creative Director**
Elayne Roberts

**Imaging**
Ralph Olmedo, Jr.

**Product Manager**
Phil Garcia

**Publishers**
Rachelle Cracchiolo, M.S. Ed.
Mary Dupuy Smith, M.S. Ed.

# How to Use Parts of Speech

## Grades 6–8

**Author**

*Toni Rouse*

***Teacher Created Materials, Inc.***
6421 Industry Way
Westminster, CA 92683
www.teachercreated.com

**ISBN-1-57690-500-5**

*©1999 Teacher Created Materials, Inc.*

Made in U.S.A.

# Table of Contents

# Table of Contents *(cont.)*

# Introduction to Teachers

*How to Use Parts of Speech* is a guide for your students to become familiar with the basic units of grammar—the parts of speech! First, an introduction with a study list of the parts of speech is provided for the student. It includes the definitions, key words, and examples. Then, each part of speech is defined, with tips for identification. Practice exercises are then provided for identifying that part of speech. Next, different usage rules and exercises are provided for practice with these concepts. A review of parts of speech identification and a review of usage are provided at the end of the book, along with a peer editing checklist for students to use with their own writing.

You may wish to introduce each part of speech and usage concept in class, do the introductory exercises together, and have the students complete the remaining exercises from each section as homework; or all work could be done in class, depending on the level of your students and their previous exposure to grammar.

Naturally, the concepts taught here are more likely to become ingrained if the ideas are reinforced in the students' other writing assignments. Peer editing is a perfect opportunity to reinforce the students' learning. The peer editing checklist is provided for this reason.

# Introduction

Welcome to the wonderful world of grammar! Grammar is about using language correctly. In order to understand grammar, we must first understand the basic units of grammar: words. Parts of speech are the different types of words that make up our language. Depending on its function in a sentence, each word is a particular part of speech. For example, nouns are words which name people, places, ideas, and things. There are seven other parts of speech as well.

Read over this study list to familiarize yourself with the eight parts of speech. This list can be used as a study guide when you've completed *How to Use Parts of Speech* and are preparing for your review.

On the following pages, in-depth explanations of each part of speech are provided, along with practice exercises to ensure full understanding.

---

## Parts of Speech Study List

**NOUN** names person, place, thing, or idea
**Key Word** "names"
**Examples** *girl, Sacramento, book, peace*

**PRONOUN** replaces noun
**Key Word** "replaces"
**Examples** *she, they, it*

**VERB** shows action or state of being
**Key Words** "action, being"
**Examples** *run, go, think, be, is*

**ADJECTIVE** describes, modifies noun or pronoun
**Key Word** "describes"
**Examples** *big, ugly, nice*

**ADVERB** describes, modifies verb, adjective, adverb
**Key Word** "describes"
**Examples** *slowly, tomorrow, very*

**PREPOSITION** shows relationship between words
**Key Word** "relationship"
**Examples** *under, on, in, by*

**CONJUNCTION** connects or joins other words
**Key Word** "connects"
**Examples** *and, but, or*

**INTERJECTION** shows strong or sudden emotion
**Key Word** "emotion"
**Examples** *Wow! Golly! Gee!*

---

# Introduction to Nouns

**NOUNS—Words that name people, places, things, or ideas**

The first part of speech is the noun. A noun is a word that names a person, place, thing, or idea: **girl**, **Cindy**, **town**, **Sacramento**, **building**, **the White House**, **peace**, **happiness**.

People, place, and thing nouns are fairly easy; you can see and touch them. Anything or anyone you can point at is a noun: **desk**, **student**, **room**, etc.

Idea nouns are invisible. They are words like **freedom**, **hatred**, **intelligence**. They seem tricky at first, but actually they're easy, too. Here is a strategy to help you identify them. Look at these words:

**happy**                    **liberty**                    **stupid**

**Liberty** is the only noun. How do you know? There's an easy test which tells you. Ask yourself, "Can I have it?" Can you have **happy**? No you can't, but you can have **happiness** or **joy**. They're nouns. Can you have **stupid**? No, but **stupidity**, **ignorance**, **intolerance**—all these you can have. This test works because all these idea nouns are things, and you can have things. You can have a pencil, a book, some apples—all things. Idea nouns are really thing nouns. They are just invisible things.

## Exercise 1

List 10 person nouns.

1. _____        6. _____
2. _____        7. _____
3. _____        8. _____
4. _____        9. _____
5. _____        10. _____

## Exercise 2

List 10 place nouns.

1. _____        6. _____
2. _____        7. _____
3. _____        8. _____
4. _____        9. _____
5. _____        10. _____

# Noun Practice

## Exercise 3

List 10 thing nouns.

1. _____     6. _____
2. _____     7. _____
3. _____     8. _____
4. _____     9. _____
5. _____     10. _____

## Exercise 4

List 10 idea nouns.

1. _____     6. _____
2. _____     7. _____
3. _____     8. _____
4. _____     9. _____
5. _____     10. _____

## Exercise 5

Write **N** next to the words that can be used as nouns. They may be person, place, thing, or idea nouns.

1. desk _____
2. friendship _____
3. dream _____
4. quirky _____
5. ship _____
6. police _____
7. coward _____
8. purple _____
9. church _____
10. religion _____
11. Ms. Garcia _____
12. United States _____
13. bookmark _____
14. *Romeo and Juliet* _____
15. tears _____
16. fear _____
17. afraid _____
18. nice _____
19. cat _____
20. hatred _____

# Capitalization Rules

Nouns which name specific persons, places, or things are called **proper nouns**, and they must be capitalized. Here are the rules for capitalizing these nouns:

## Nationalities, Religions

1. Capitalize all nationalities and religions: Protestant, Italian, Jewish, Australian.

## Dates

2. Capitalize dates, historical events, periods, and special events: World War II, Renaissance, Boston Tea Party, Easter, Saturday, May.

3. Do not capitalize seasons of the year: winter, spring, autumn, summer.

## Classes

4. Do not capitalize school classes unless a specific title is given, or the subject is a language: history, History 1A, English, Spanish, geometry.

## Names

5. Capitalize names of people and place names: Ron, Atlanta, Nevada, Mexico, Main Street, Ms. Rafferty.

   **Note:** Do not capitalize directions (south, east, etc.) except when they refer to a specific region (the South): I live north of the capital. We moved to the East Coast.

6. Capitalize titles for people (mayor, doctor, president) only when they are followed by a name (Doctor Stockton, the doctor).

7. Capitalize the first and last words and all important words in the titles of books, stories, poems, songs, etc.: *A Tree Grows in Brooklyn*, "Once in a Lifetime."

8. Capitalize family titles only when used as names: Ask Mom. Ask your mom. I like Uncle Bob. I like my uncle, Bob.

9. Capitalize the names of organizations, businesses, institutions, and government bodies: Central High School, Imation Enterprises Corporation, Food and Drug Administration, United States Navy.

10. Capitalize the brand names of products but not the words identifying the products: Dove soap, Nike shoes.

11. Capitalize the names of planets, ships, awards, monuments, and any other specific places, things, or events: *Titanic*, Venus, Mars, the White House, Academy Awards.

12. Capitalize words referring to God: God loves His people.

    **Note:** Do not capitalize the word *god* when referring to deities: The Greek gods lived on Mount Olympus.

## The Obvious Ones

13. Capitalize the first word in every sentence.

14. Capitalize the pronoun *I* and the interjection *O*.

# Capitalization Practice

**Exercise 1:** Mark *A* if the underlined word is correct as it is, and mark *B* if it is incorrect.

b Z D V q E u S P

A

_____ 1. My <u>Aunt</u> is named Terry.

q

_____ 2. I like <u>Aunt</u> Terry.

u

_____ 3. Sit by your <u>Cousin,</u> Tommy.

y

W

_____ 4. I don't want to sit by <u>Cousin</u> Tommy.

k

_____ 5. I come from the <u>west</u>.

T

_____ 6. I live <u>west</u> of the river.

j

_____ 7. I like <u>spanish</u> class.

e

_____ 8. I like <u>math</u> class.

L

_____ 9. My favorite season is <u>Fall</u>.

i

_____ 10. Is the <u>Mayor</u> in?

c

B

_____ 11. Yes, <u>Mayor</u> Ruiz is in.

e

_____ 12. The <u>President</u> of General Motors is rich.

r

_____ 13. <u>President</u> Kennedy lived in the White House.

P

_____ 14. My mother is <u>christian</u>.

P

_____ 15. I like <u>History</u> 101.

A

a W K O S Q Z g t

x

# More Capitalization Practice

**Exercise 2:** Mark *A* for correct (no capitalization errors in the sentence), and mark *B* for incorrect (the sentence contains an error or errors in capitalization).

_____ 1. Sea Kayaking at Elkhorn Slough is fun!

_____ 2. John can't wait until he graduates from High School.

_____ 3. I only use Ivory Soap on my face.

_____ 4. My friend lives east of here.

_____ 5. I grew up in the south.

_____ 6. I don't know whether my mom can give us a ride or not.

_____ 7. Most students like their Math classes.

_____ 8. All students like their english classes.

_____ 9. I love Autumn weather!

_____10. We will meet on tuesday of next week.

_____11. I'll ask dad if he can fix it.

_____12. My doctor said I shouldn't eat peanuts.

_____13. Did you vote for president Clinton?

_____14. Who is the president of Pepsico?

_____15. I enjoy Lay's potato chips.

_____16. We're studying the Civil War in history class.

_____17. I hope we get to visit the Lincoln memorial in Washington, D.C.

_____18. I met him on a Monday during the Summer.

_____19. Do you have any kleenex?

_____20. I think this case may go to the supreme court.

# Possessives

**Possessive nouns** show possession or ownership of the noun(s) following them:

**Laura's** house          **Bill's** lunch          the **children's** books     the **actors'** costumes

Here are the rules for forming the possessive forms of nouns:

1.  To form the possessive of a singular noun, add an apostrophe and an *s*:

| **Singular Noun** | **Possessive Form** |
| :---: | :---: |
| Ms. Bucco | Ms. Bucco's |
| waiter | waiter's |
| Charles | Charles's |

**Note:** When a name ends in an *s* (like Charles), you only have to put an apostrophe after the *s* that already ends the name to make it a possessive. However, it's always correct to add an apostrophe and an *s* to any possessive singular noun. So, either is correct: Charles' or Charles's.

2.  To form the possessive of a plural noun that ends in *s*, just add an apostrophe after the *s*. This shows that the *s* is doing two jobs: making the noun plural and making it possessive.

| **Plural Noun** | **Possessive Form** |
| :---: | :---: |
| teams | teams' |
| waiters | waiters' |
| dogs | dogs' |

3.  To form the possessive of a plural noun that does not end in *s*, add an apostrophe and an *s*, just like you would if the noun were singular.

| **Plural Noun** | **Possessive Form** |
| :---: | :---: |
| children | children's |
| women | women's |
| sheep | sheep's |

Here's an easy way to know how to form a possessive when you are writing a sentence. Write the word you need for the sentence (as a singular or a plural). To make it possessive when the word has an *s* at the end already, add an apostrophe after the *s*; if the word does not have an *s* at the end, add an apostrophe and then an *s*. This always works.

**Note:** Apostrophes are used for two other reasons:

1.  To show that letters or numbers have been left out:

    she'll (The apostrophe shows that the *wi* has been left out of *she will.*)

    '99 (The apostrophe shows that the *19* has been left out of *1999.*)

2.  To show the plural of numbers and letters.

    I got two *A's.*

    There are four *5's* in this equation.

# Possessives Practice

**Name**_____

**Exercise 1:** To complete each sentence, form the possessive of the noun in parentheses. If the noun is singular, keep it singular. If it is plural, keep it plural.

1. The _____ lounge is upstairs. (teachers)

2. Our _____ motto is "E Pluribus Unum." (country)

3. The _____ department is on the third floor. (children)

4. _____ friends are coming to dinner. (Ross)

5. Where's the _____ room? (men)

6. All the _____ leaders were there. (cities)

7. All the _____ dishes are empty. (dogs)

8. _____ dish is full. (Argus)

9. That's _____ van. (Karla)

10. The _____ practice ends at 3:00. (girls)

**Exercise 2:** Mark *A* if the underlined word is correct, and mark *B* if it is incorrect.

_____ 1. That's the <u>ladies'</u> room.

_____ 2. I have five <u>cat's</u>.

_____ 3. That <u>babies'</u> mother is Marion.

_____ 4. Our <u>team's</u> mascot is the bulldog.

_____ 5. The <u>mens</u> locker room is closed.

_____ 6. I like old <u>cars</u>.

_____ 7. <u>Chris'</u> mother is bringing lunch.

_____ 8. That <u>ladie's</u> purse is huge.

_____ 9. Your <u>binder's</u> pocket is ripped.

_____ 10. My <u>baby's</u> room is too hot.

# Introduction to Pronouns

| PRONOUNS—Words that take the place of nouns |
|---|

Why do we need pronouns? Without pronouns, we'd sound like this:

Mary drove Mary's car to Mary's boyfriend's house to take Mary's boyfriend to the movie. Mary and Mary's boyfriend enjoyed the movie. Mary and Mary's boyfriend said the movie was exciting.

With pronouns, we can say this:

Mary drove **her** car to **her** boyfriend's house to take **him** to the movie. **They** enjoyed the movie. **They** said **it** was exciting.

Pronouns keep us from having to repeat the same nouns over and over.

Pronouns are a simple part of speech. They are words like **she**, **he**, **him**, **they**, **us**, **we**, and **it**. They are words that can replace specific nouns. Every noun can be replaced by a pronoun.

## Exercise 1

Underline the pronouns in the following sentences.

1. The cat ate her dinner.
2. The students brought their books.
3. I have a new car, and it is pretty.
4. We aren't going to the party.
5. Are you going with us?

6. That is a nice painting.
7. This is my favorite book.
8. I like the new teacher; she is nice.
9. Naomi brought her lunch.
10. That is a good idea. I like it.

**Note:** Hopefully, you noticed that, like nouns, pronouns have possessive forms; however, unlike nouns, pronouns usually do not form the possessives with an apostrophe and an *s*. Instead, they change form. Here are some examples of pronouns and their possessive forms:

*He* becomes *his*.

*She* becomes *hers* or *her*.

*They* becomes *their*.

*I* becomes *my* or *mine*.

*It* becomes *its*.

## Exercise 2

First, write a journal entry in which you tell what you did when you got home from school yesterday. Do not use any pronouns. Remember that *I* and *me* are pronouns! Next, rewrite the entry, adding pronouns where they are appropriate.

# Agreement of Pronoun and Antecedent

What is an **antecedent**? An antecedent is the word to which a pronoun refers.

Betty brought her book to class.

In this sentence, *her* is the only pronoun. Its antecedent is *Betty* because *Betty* is the word to which the pronoun refers. When we talk about pronoun-antecedent agreement, we mean that pronouns must agree in number and gender with their antecedents. If Betty is the antecedent, we couldn't say, "Betty brought *his* book," or "Betty brought *their* book." In those sentences, the pronouns don't agree with their antecedents.

The only time this gets tricky is when we use the indefinite pronouns. These are indefinite pronouns:

*one, everyone, someone, no one, anyone, everybody, nobody, anybody, somebody, each, either, neither, several, few, both, many, all, most, any, none.*

Here are the rules about using indefinite pronouns properly so that the pronoun and antecedent agree:

1. These indefinite pronouns are singular and therefore take a singular antecedent: *one, everyone, someone, no one, anyone, everybody, nobody, anybody, somebody, each, either, neither.*

It's easy to remember most of these because most of them end in either *one* or *body*, and we know that *one* and *body* are singular.

Everybody has his or her book.

**Note:** In the above sentence, many people would use the word *their* in place of *his or her*. This is incorrect because *everybody* is a singular pronoun which is not gender specific. Many people prefer to use the male pronoun *his* when referring to all of us. This is still considered acceptable grammar. Nowadays, however, we generally say *his or her* so that we have a singular pronoun and are not being gender-biased.

2. These indefinite pronouns are **plural** and therefore take **plural antecedents**: *several, few, both, many*.

*Several* students lost their books.

*Many* of us have taken our tests.

3. These indefinite pronouns may be either singular or plural, depending on how they are used in a sentence: *all, most, any, none.*

*Most* of the apples are rotten. (plural)

*Most* of the milk is gone. (singular)

**Note:** If a sentence has a **compound antecedent** (more than one) joined by *or* or *nor*, the pronoun agrees with the antecedent closer to it.

Either the girls or Jose brought *his* car.

Either Jose or the girls brought *their* car.

# Pronoun-Antecedent Agreement Practice

**Name**_____

## Exercise 1

Underline the pronouns that agree with their antecedents.

1. Nobody brought (their/his or her) jacket.

2. Some of the students raised (their/his or her) hands.

3. Each of the girls took (their/her) turn.

4. Either the boys or Cindy will volunteer (their/her) time.

5. Someone left (their/his or her) gloves.

6. Neither Bob or Jack brought (their/his) shoes.

7. Most of the kids like (their/his or her) teacher.

8. Everybody must ask (their/his or her) parents for permission.

9. Many of the teachers drove (their/his or her) cars.

10. One of the boys lost (their/his) book.

11. Somebody should raise (their/his or her) hand.

12. Nobody dropped (their/his or her) cards.

13. Bob and Jose lost (their/his) pencils.

14. Maria or Cindy brought (their/her) car.

15. Anybody who likes grammar should raise (their/his or her) hand.

# Subject and Object Pronouns

Personal pronouns have two forms: the subject and the object forms.

| Subject | Object |
|---------|--------|
| I | me |
| she | her |
| he | him |
| they | them |
| we | us |

As you can see, the pronouns on the left mean exactly the same thing as the pronouns on the right. For example, *I* and *me* mean the same thing. The difference is that the pronouns on the left are used when they are acting as subjects, and the pronouns on the right are used when acting as objects. This sounds difficult, but there's an easy way to figure out how to use the correct form.

Usually we use the correct form automatically. For example, we wouldn't say, "Me like you." We would say, "I like you." *I* is the subject. Sometimes, though, when another person is added to the sentence, we are unsure. For example, which is correct?

Go to the store with Bob and *I*.

Go to the store with Bob and *me*.

The second sentence is correct. An easy way to test this is to eliminate the other person in the sentence and say the sentence with the pronoun by itself. Here, we would say, "Go to the store with me." We wouldn't say "Go to the store with I." Therefore, *me* is the correct form of the pronoun for this sentence, even if we add another person.

## Exercise 1

Underline the correct pronoun(s) for each sentence.

1. Bob and (I, me) are going.
2. Stand by the captain and (I, me).
3. (We, Us) girls are going to win.
4. Are Sandy and (she, her) going?
5. You and (he, him) make a cute couple.
6. I'm going to the party with Fred and (they, them).
7. If Lucia and (they, them) go, I'm not going.
8. Give the papers to (she, her) and (we, us) before you leave.
9. You can't play with (we, us) boys.
10. If you go with Ranvir and (I, me), we will have more fun.

# Subject and Object Pronoun Practice

**Name** _____

**Exercise 2:** Underline the correct pronouns from the choices given in the following sentences.

1. (We, Us) teachers are going on vacation together.

2. You may go with (we, us) teachers.

3. My sister and (I, me) are going to visit Grandma.

4. She can't go with (he, him) and (she, her).

5. They and (we, us) all did well on the project.

6. My father sent Debbie and (I, me) a card.

7. The teacher wrote detentions for (he, him) and (I, me).

8. A package arrived for (we, us) kids.

9. Don't hold this against Nicki and (I, me).

10. The teacher called on (he, him) and (she, her).

11. We are going to have pizza with the boys and (she, her).

12. (He, Him) and (I, me) are going out to dinner.

13. There was a tie between (she, her) and (he, him).

14. (He, Him) and the clerk got into an argument.

15. (They, Them) and the girls are following us.

16. The students and (I, me) are having a good day.

17. (We, Us) and (they, them) are playing the final match.

18. I wrote a letter to (he, him) and (she, her).

19. I like to ride with John and (she, her).

20. The principal was staring at (they, them) and (we, us).

# Introduction to Verbs

| **VERBS—Words that show action or state of being** |
| --- |

Action verbs are easy. They're *doing* words. To find the action verb in a sentence, you ask this about the subject: "What is she/he/it doing?"

Jose rode the bus.

What is Jose doing? *Riding!* That's the verb—in this case *rode*, past tense. Here are some more examples:

1. The cat eats a lot.
2. The baby fell down the stairs.
3. Jane yelled.

What are the subjects in each sentence doing (or what have they done)?

1. eats
2. fell
3. yelled

The other kind of verbs are called *state of being* or *linking verbs*. They don't show action; they link the subject of the sentence to a word that describes the subject or a word that renames the subject. This sounds difficult, but actually it's quite simple.

Jane is pretty.

We know the subject is Jane, but what is she doing? She's doing nothing. She just *is*. She's just being pretty. *Is* is the verb. It links the subject, *Jane*, with a word describing her, *pretty*. We can also link her to a word that renames her:

Jane is the captain.

The most common linking verbs are forms of the word *be*:

*is, are, was, am, be, been, being*

Some verbs can be action or linking verbs, depending on how they are used in a sentence. Look at the verbs in these sentences:

She felt sick.<br>She felt the baby's forehead.

In the first sentence, *felt* is a linking verb. It's linking *she* with *sick*, a word describing her. In the second, *felt* is an action verb. It's showing what she's doing. It's not linking her to anything. It's not saying she *is* the baby's forehead! See if you can tell when the verb *smelled* in the next sentences is used as an action verb and when it is used as a linking verb.

Bob smelled the flowers.<br>Bob smelled nice.

The first is action, and the second is linking. In the first sentence, *smelled* is what Bob did. It's an action. Bob is not being linked to anything. It's not saying that Bob *is* the flowers. In the second sentence, *smelled* is not an action or doing word. It's linking *Bob* to a describing word: *nice*.

18

# Verb Practice

**Name**_____

**Exercise 1:** Underline the verb(s) in each sentence.

1. Ms. Davis talks a lot.

2. She is talkative.

3. I ran into the door.

4. We read *Sounder*.

5. I enjoyed it.

6. I think about *Sounder* all the time.

7. I hope we get other good books this year.

8. I like all kinds of books.

9. I had a root canal yesterday.

10. The dentist was nice.

**Exercise 2:** Underline the verb in each sentence. If the verb is an action verb, mark *A* after the sentence, and if it is a linking verb, mark *L* at the end of the sentence.

1. Ms. Oudegeest plays with her computer.

2. She also watches TV.

3. She likes *Friends*.

4. Max looks mad.

5. He spit at the dog.

6. Spitting is gross.

7. The dog seems mad now.

8. Karla looked out the window.

9. She saw her dad.

10. Her dad is her best friend.

11. Cathy Lew asked for our attention on the intercom.

12. We heard her very well.

13. She sounded funny, though.

14. Cathy Lew is really nice.

15. Students and teachers like her.

# More Verb Practice

**Name**_____

**Exercise 3:** Underline the verb in each sentence.

1. The cat ran under the table.
2. She coughed up a hairball.
3. We rode to school on the bus.
4. Please throw your gum away.
5. The bell will ring in three minutes.

6. My dog ate my homework.
7. I bought three Twinkies.
8. Don't write on my paper.
9. I'll borrow some paper from Mimi.
10. Did you see *Titanic*?

**Exercise 4:** For each of the verbs listed in the box below, write two sentences. In the first sentence, use the verb as a linking verb, and in the second, use it is an action verb. **Note:** You may use any form of the verb you wish (past, present, future, etc.)

**Example:** sound

1. That song *sounds* cool. (L)
2. Quasimodo *sounded* the bell. (A)

| | |
|---|---|
| a. appear | d. grow |
| b. feel | e. look |
| c. smell | |

_____

_____

_____

_____

_____

_____

_____

_____

# The Principal Parts of Verbs

The four basic forms of a verb are called the *principal* parts. Study these carefully.

1. The four principal parts of a verb are the *infinitive, present participle, past,* and *past participle.*

| Infinitive | Present Participle | Past | Past Participle |
|------------|--------------------|------|-----------------|
| ring | (is) ringing | rang | (has) rung |

The present participle and past participle forms are used with helping verbs like *am, is, are, has, have,* etc. A *participle* is a verb that can be used as an adjective.

The *pouring* rain drove us inside.

*Waxed* floors can be very slippery.

The floor was littered with *broken* toys.

2. A verb that forms its past and past participle forms by adding *-d* or *-ed* to the infinitive is a regular verb.

| Infinitive | Present Participle | Past | Past Participle |
|------------|--------------------|------|-----------------|
| use | (is) using | used | (has) used |

3. A verb that forms its past and past participle in some other way is an *irregular verb.* You may have noticed that *ring* is an irregular verb.

Usually, we don't have too many problems with verb tense. The most common problem we have is figuring when to use the past form and when to use the past participle form with irregular verbs. For example, we might say, "I seen that movie." This is incorrect because *seen* is the past participle form of the verb *see.* Therefore, *seen* should only be used with a helping verb. On the next page is a handy list of some common irregular verbs which are often troublesome.

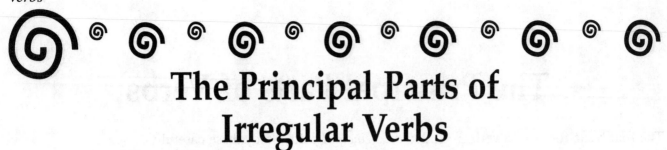

# The Principal Parts of Irregular Verbs

Remember that the past tense does not use a helping verb and the past participle does use a helping verb. **Note:** The present participle form has been left off this list because it isn't troublesome; it's just the infinitive form with *-ing* added. Review this list carefully.

| Infinitive | Past | Past Participle | Infinitive | Past | Past Participle |
|---|---|---|---|---|---|
| become | became | become | lie | lay | lain |
| begin | began | begun | ride | rode | ridden |
| bite | bit | bitten | ring | rang | rung |
| blow | blew | blown | rise | rose | risen |
| break | broke | broken | run | ran | run |
| bring | brought | brought | see | saw | seen |
| burst | burst | burst | set | set | set |
| buy | bought | bought | shake | shook | shaken |
| catch | caught | caught | shine* | shone | shone |
| choose | chose | chosen | shrink | shrank | shrunk |
| climb | climbed | climbed | sing | sang | sung |
| come | came | come | sink | sank | sunk |
| do | did | done | sit | sat | sat |
| drag | dragged | dragged | speak | spoke | spoken |
| draw | drew | drawn | spring | sprang | sprung |
| drink | drank | drunk | steal | stole | stolen |
| drive | drove | driven | swear | swore | sworn |
| drown | drowned | drowned | swim | swam | swum |
| eat | ate | eaten | take | took | taken |
| fall | fell | fallen | tear | tore | torn |
| fly | flew | flown | throw | threw | thrown |
| freeze | froze | frozen | wear | wore | worn |
| give | gave | given | write | wrote | written |
| go | went | gone | | | |
| grow | grew | grown | | | |
| know | knew | known | | | |
| lay | laid | laid | | | |

*When *shine* means *polish*, the parts are *shine, shined, shined.*

# Verb Form Practice

**Name**_____

**Exercise 1:** Underline the correct verb form from the choices given.

1. I should have (knew/known) that I could have (froze/frozen) my toes.

2. As soon as Manuel had (chose/chosen) his subject, he (began/begun) his talk.

3. The coat that I had (wore/worn) only once had been (stole/stolen).

4. The dress that I would have (chose/chosen) was (tore/torn).

5. Has the bell (rang/rung), or would I (have/of) heard it here?

6. The man who had (stole/stolen) the money was (knew/known) by the police.

7. You should (have/of) known that the song was (sang/sung) by Marilyn.

8. Has he always (drove/driven) so carelessly, or has he just (began/begun) to do so?

9. She (began/begun) to see that she had (chose/chosen) the wrong topic.

10. Snow (fell/fallen) after the pond had (froze/frozen).

11. Our doorbell is (wore/worn) out because the children have (rang/rung) it too many times.

12. Two cups have (fell/fallen) off the shelf and have (broke/broken).

13. Barbara (sang/sung) the song that was (chose/chosen) by the committee.

14. I would have (brung/brought) my stereo if it hadn't been (stole/stolen).

15. The telephone (rang/rung) just as I (began/begun) to study.

# Introduction to Adjectives

---

**ADJECTIVES—Words that describe nouns and pronouns**

---

Adjectives describe nouns. They can also describe pronouns because pronouns take the place of nouns. Usually, we find adjectives in front of the nouns or pronouns they are describing.

### That's a blue car.

(*Blue* is an adjective describing the noun *car.*)

### She's a nice girl.

(*Nice* is an adjective describing the noun *girl.*)

We also find adjectives in sentences like the ones discussed in the verb section, in which a linking verb is linking the subject of the sentence to a word that describes the subject. The describing word is an adjective since a subject has to be a noun or pronoun, and adjectives are the only words that describe nouns or pronouns.

### Cindy looks pretty.

(*Pretty* is an adjective describing the noun *Cindy.*)

### She is smart.

(*Smart* is an adjective describing the pronoun *she.*)

**Exercise 1:** Underline the adjective(s) in the following sentences. Beside each sentence, write the adjective(s) plus the noun(s) being described.

1. The big truck hit the little car. _____

2. That's a good book. _____

3. My cute kitty is washing her sweet face. _____

4. Ms. Bronowski is nice. _____

5. My dad made a delicious cake. _____

6. That's a silly thing to say. _____

7. I like chocolate ice cream. _____

8. I like the red car better than the blue one. _____

9. This book is old. _____

10. Here's a shiny new penny! _____

# Adjective Practice

**Name**_____

**Exercise 1:** Underline the adjective(s) in the following sentences. Beside each sentence, write the adjective(s) plus the noun(s) being described.

1. The red car has a flat tire. _____

2. Sherry is an early bird._____

3. The sheep went into their empty shed. _____

4. Our old car needs new brakes._____

5. Max cooked a hot, peppery sauce. _____

6. The fat, laughing clown led the parade. _____

7. Black soot coated the fireplace._____

8. The Dutch windmill made a screechy sound. _____

9. A young otter splashed in the small pond. _____

10. The dynamic speaker excited the large crowd. _____

**Exercise 2:** Rewrite the following sentences, adding at least one adjective to each. Underline the adjectives you add.

1. I brought a car. _____

2. Suzy is my friend. _____

3. Ms. Rouse is our teacher._____

4. I ate my lunch. _____

5. I read that book. _____

6. Dogs are running after us! _____

7. You are a football player. _____

8. The 49ers beat the Rams._____

9. My sister threw the ball. _____

10. That is my cat. _____

# Degrees of Adjectives

As we know, adjectives describe nouns or pronouns:

*sandy* beach

*high* score

Adjectives can also be used to compare one noun or pronoun to another:

That's a *sandier* beach than the other.

His was the *highest* score in the class.

Adjectives have three forms: the *positive*, the *comparative*, and the *superlative*. The positive is the regular form of the adjective. It is used to describe a noun. The comparative and superlative forms are used for comparison. When comparing two things, people, or places, use the comparative form. This is usually formed by adding *-er* to the positive form or by inserting the word *more* in front of the positive form if the adjective has two syllables or more and doesn't end with a *y*. When comparing more than two people, places, or things, use the superlative form. This is usually formed by adding *-est* to the adjective or by inserting the word *most* in front of the adjective if the adjective has two or more syllables and doesn't end with a *y*. Some words are irregular and do not follow a pattern for making their comparative and superlative forms. For example, we don't use *good, gooder,* or *goodest*. We use *good, better,* and *best*.

| Positive | Comparative | Superlative |
|:---:|:---:|:---:|
| *(describes one)* | *(compares two)* | *(compares three or more)* |
| short | shorter | shortest |
| careful | more careful | most careful |
| bad | worse | worst |
| good | better | best |
| hairy | hairier | hairiest |
| smart | smarter | smartest |
| high | higher | highest |
| silly | sillier | silliest |
| fun | more fun | most fun |
| young | younger | youngest |

# Adjective Degree Practice

Name_____

**Exercise 1:** Write the correct form of the adjective given for each sentence.

1. That is the _____ movie I have ever seen. (*bad*)

2. Ella has the _____ record of anyone. (*good*)

3. Of the two poems, Sarah's is _____. (*good*)

4. My cold is _____ than Tom's. (*bad*)

5. Jane is the _____ student in class. (*smart*)

6. Which of your feet is _____? (*short*)

7. That was the _____ rally I've ever attended. (*exciting*)

8. Which of you two is _____? (*young*)

9. I will be _____ than Max. (*careful*)

10. That's the _____ cat I've ever seen. (*hairy*)

11. Of you two, I hope the _____ man wins. (*good*)

12. Who is _____, Jan or Marsha? (*smart*)

13. We won the basketball game because we had the _____ score. (*high*)

14. Who has the _____ score in class? (*high*)

15. Marta is the _____ of the twins. (*silly*)

# Introduction to Adverbs

---

**ADVERBS—Words that describe verbs, adjectives, and other adverbs**

---

Adverbs describe verbs. That's easy to remember because the word *verb* is part of the word *adverb*. Adverbs also describe adjectives and other adverbs.

Usually adverbs are describing verbs.

We ate fast.

(Fast is an adverb describing the verb ate.)

He speaks quietly.

Note: Adverbs often end in -ly.

(Quietly is an adverb describing the verb speaks.)

Adverbs answer these questions: How? When? Where?

Bob walked quickly.

(How did Bob walk?)

Bob walked yesterday.

(When did Bob walk?)

Bob walked upstairs.

(Where did Bob walk?)

It is difficult to come up with many adverbs that answer Where? That's okay. There just happen to be many more adverbs that answer How? than any others.

**Note:** You might have noticed that phrases like *down the street* act as adverbs. For now, however, we'll stick to single-word adverbs.

Here are some adverbs that describe adjectives and other adverbs.

He is really nice.

(Really is an adverb describing the adjective nice. How nice is he? He is really nice.)

That's an extremely fast car.

(Extremely is an adverb describing the adjective fast. How fast? Extremely fast.)

You read very well.

(Very is an adverb describing the adverb well. How well? Very well.)

When adverbs are describing adjectives or other adverbs, they are usually words like *very*, but they can also be the opposite.

You are not nice.

(Not is an adverb describing the adjective nice. How nice? Not nice at all.)

# Adverb Practice

**Name**_____

**Exercise 1:** Add adverbs which answer how, where, or when about the verbs in the following sentences.  Underline the adverbs you add.  Use a different adverb for each sentence.

   a. They eat.  They eat <u>loudly</u>.
      b. She wrote a letter.  She <u>quickly</u> wrote a letter.
      c. I fell.  I fell <u>downstairs</u>.

1. Theresa threw the ball._____

2. We read the story. _____

3. We flew down the street. _____

4. He ate the pizza._____

5. Bob hiccupped in class. _____

6. The mummy walked. _____

7. Students talked. _____

8. We watched the news program._____

9. The teacher listened. _____

10. My friends sat under the tree. _____

**Exercise 2:** Add adverbs to modify the adjectives or other adverbs already in these sentences.  Underline the adverbs you add.  Do not use the same adverb more than once.

**Note:** When adverbs are used to describe other describing words, they can be called *intensifiers*.

   a. John is nice.  John is <u>quite</u> nice.
      b. You drive fast.  You drive <u>too</u> fast.
      c. That's not pretty.  That's <u>really</u> not pretty.

1. Your cat is cute. _____

2. That's a wonderful book. _____

3. I bought a blue truck._____

4. You sing beautifully. _____

5. I talk quietly. _____

# More Adverb Practice

**Exercise 3:** Fill in adverbs to complete the sentences. Try not use the same adverb more than once.

1. Amanda _____ ate her popcorn.

2. Mom drives _____ carefully.

3. That vase is _____ pretty.

4. Your book fell _____ .

5. I fell asleep _____ .

6. The dog jumped _____ high.

7. Class was _____ interesting.

8. After dinner, we will _____ watch some TV.

9. Jessica is _____ smart.

10. Lydia rode the horse _____ .

11. Curtis runs _____ .

12. You type _____ .

13. That's a _____ weird picture.

14. We slept _____ soundly.

15. The teacher lectured _____ .

16. I will call you _____ .

17. Don't yell _____ loudly!

18. Grandma likes to read _____ .

19. This is a _____ good book.

20. My niece can sing _____ .

30

# Modifier Practice

**Name**_____

Adjectives and adverbs are called *modifiers* because they are the describing words. They modify or describe other words. **Adverbs and *adjectives* add to other words.**

As we know, adjectives can only describe nouns and pronouns.

Fran is nice. (*nice* describes the noun *Fran*)

That is an ugly car. (*ugly* describes the noun *car*)

I got a good grade. (*good* describes the noun *grade*)

She is smart. (*smart* describes the pronoun *she*)

Adverbs describe verbs, adjectives, and other adverbs. When they do this, they are always answering one of these questions about the words they are describing: How? When? Where?

Here are some adverbs describing verbs:

John eats noisily. (*noisily* describes **how** John eats—*eats* is a verb)

Cindy ran upstairs. (*upstairs* describes **where** she ran—*ran* is a verb)

Our team won yesterday. (*yesterday* describes **when** they won—*won* is a verb)

As we know, adverbs also describe adjectives and other adverbs. In other words, adverbs describe describing words. Any describing word we can think of can be described some more by an adverb.

I got a really good grade. (*really* describes how good the grade was—*good* is an adjective describing the noun *grade*, so *really* is an adverb describing an adjective)

John eats extremely *noisily*. (*extremely* describes how noisily John eats—*noisily* is an adverb describing the verb *eats*, so *extremely* is an adverb describing an adverb)

**Exercise 1:** Underline the adjectives and adverbs in the following sentences. Label them, and then draw a line to the word each is describing.

**adv adj**

Example A:  You're quite silly.

**adj**

Example B:  I can hear the noisy stereo.

1. That's a very nice car you have.
2. She writes very well.
3. Dina sings really badly.

4. This paper is barely readable.
5. Karla really likes crispy cookies.

**Exercise 2:** On the other side of this paper, write five sentences in which adverbs are used to describe adjectives. Label each.

**adv  adj**

Bob has a *really nice* car.

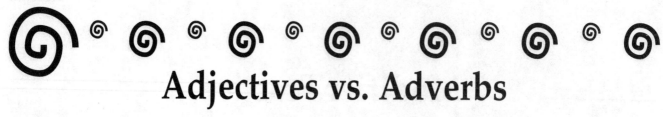

# Adjectives vs. Adverbs

It's important to know the difference between adverbs and adjectives in order to use them correctly. There are some sets of adjectives and adverbs which are troublesome. Here are some rules to help with those sets.

1. **Good vs. Well**

   *Good* is an adjective used to describe nouns and pronouns.

   This is a good essay.<br>The children were good today.

   *Well* can also be an adjective when it is used to mean *healthy*. It follows a linking verb and describes the noun or pronoun in front of the linking verb.

   I am feeling well today.<br>You don't look well.

   *Well* is most often used as an adverb to describe verbs, adjectives, and other adverbs.

   You write well.<br>The teacher is well read.

2. **Bad vs. Badly**

   *Bad* is an adjective used to describe nouns and pronouns. It often follows linking verbs and describes the noun or pronoun in front of the linking verb.

   I feel bad today.<br>This milk tastes bad.

   *Badly* is an adverb which is used to describe verbs, adjectives, and other adverbs.

   Joey hit the ball badly.<br>That is a badly damaged car.

3. **Real vs. Really**

   *Real* is an adjective which means *true* or *actual*. It describes nouns and pronouns.

   Is this a real gold piece?<br>Which of these stories is real?

   *Really* is an adverb usually used as an intensifier to describe adjectives and other adverbs. It can also be used to mean *actually* when describing verbs.

   That's a really nice outfit.<br>Are you really going?

**Note:** It is not correct to use *real* as follows:

This is a real great party.

The proper sentence is . . .

This is a really great party.

# Adjectives vs. Adverbs Practice

**Name** _____

**Exercise 1:** Fill in each blank with the proper word from the choices given.

1. We had a _____ time. (good, well)

2. Do you feel _____ ? (good, well)

3. That cake looks really _____ . (good, well)

4. I can't run very _____ . (good, well)

5. You don't look _____ . Would you like to see the nurse? (good, well)

6. I feel _____ about what I said to Mom. (bad, badly)

7. I don't think I sang too _____ . (bad, badly)

8. If you feel _____ , you should apologize. (bad, badly)

9. This is a _____ movie. (bad, badly)

10. This man lectures _____ . (bad, badly)

11. Is this your _____ birth certificate? (real, really)

12. I _____ like your dad. (real, really)

13. He's _____ nice. (real, really)

14. You should read this. It's a _____ good book. (real, really)

15. Are you _____ going with her? (real, really)

16. After eating a whole pizza, I didn't feel so _____ . (good, well)

17. You're really throwing _____ now. (good, well)

18. You look _____ . (bad, badly)

19. I don't feel so _____ anymore. (bad, badly)

20. This is a _____ good movie. (real, really)

# Introduction to Prepositions

| **PREPOSITIONS—Words that show a relationship between other words** |
| --- |

To see how prepositions work, look at these two words:

**fox   log**

Prepositions can show the relationship between the fox and the log:

The fox was *under* the log.

The fox was *on* the log.

The fox was *by* the log.

The fox was *in* the log.

Prepositions always start *prepositional phrases*. A *phrase* is a group of words that doesn't make a whole sentence—a group of words that do a job together. These are all prepositional phrases:

*under the log, on the log, by the log, in the log*

Prepositional phrases always begin with a preposition and end with the *object of the preposition*. The object of the preposition is a word that answers What? or Whom? about the preposition. Under what? *The log*. On what? *The log*. In all the above prepositional phrases, *log* is the object of the preposition.

Here is a list of common prepositions:

| | | | | |
| --- | --- | --- | --- | --- |
| aboard | before | down | of | to |
| about | behind | during | off | toward |
| above | below | except | on | under |
| across | beneath | for | onto | underneath |
| after | beside | from | out | until |
| against | besides | in | outside | up |
| along | between | inside | over | upon |
| among | beyond | into | past | with |
| around | but | like | through | within |
| at | by | near | throughout | without |

Prepositions can also be made up of more than one word. These are called *compound prepositions*. Here are some common compound prepositions:

| | | |
| --- | --- | --- |
| according to | in addition to | next to |
| aside from | in front of | on account of |
| as of | in spite of | out of |
| because of | instead of | prior to |

# Preposition Practice

**Name**_____

**Exercise 1:** Under each sentence, copy the prepositional phrase from that sentence. Circle the object of the preposition and underline the preposition.

1. Penguins live at the South Pole.

   _____

2. The students slept during the speech.

   _____

3. The baby was tossed out with the bathwater.

   _____

4. The fish in the pan smelled awful.

   _____

5. The announcer on TV was excited.

   _____

6. I found the keys under the table.

   _____

7. We are going to the movies tomorrow.

   _____

8. The rabbit ran across the road.

   _____

9. Jim put the pizza on the table.

   _____

10. The girls climbed to the top.

    _____

**Exercise 2:** Rewrite each sentence, adding a prepositional phrase to each.

1. The dog ate his dinner._____

   _____

2. The boys ran. _____

   _____

3. Josh did his work. _____

   _____

4. Sally read the book. _____

   _____

5. The girls are practicing. _____

   _____

# More Preposition Practice

**Exercise 3:** World's Longest Sentence

Write **one** sentence in which you use as many prepositional phrases as you can. Underline each prepositional phrase. The following page features some sentences written by students. This will give you some ideas.

# World's Longest Sentences

Across the seas,
below the deepest ocean,
around the world and back,
beneath the earth's surface,
over the highest mountain,
toward the sky,
off the face,
of the earth,
outside of our atmosphere,
upon the highest clouds,
through all the galaxies,
beyond the farthest star,
inside my brain, and
within my heart
is where my dream lives.

Over the couch,
under the table,
behind the chair,
out the door,
across the lawn,
into the backyard,
through the swing set,
behind the tree,
over the fence,
into the alley,
beyond my sight,
on the neighbor's property,
throughout the night,
without end, and
for too little money,
I chase the kids.

In my car
across the street,
over the hills,
around the pot holes,
on the lawn,
between the garbage cans,
underneath the bridge

through the woods, and
on the sidewalk
with two wheels
underneath the garbage truck,
behind an old lady,
behind another slow car, and
after an hour,
I finally made it to school.

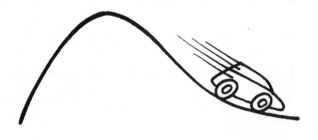

# Introduction to Conjunctions

---

**CONJUNCTIONS—Words that join or connect other words**

---

Conjunctions connect other words. It's easy to remember the definition if you emphasize it this way: **con**junctions **con**nect words.

Conjunctions are words like *and, but,* and *or.* They connect words or groups of words.

I want a car or a truck.

I want to eat dinner and go to the movies.

I like Bob, but my mom doesn't care for him.

*And, but,* and *or* are the most commonly used conjunctions. There are others, though, including *if, so, although, since,* and *because.*

You may go to the party if you clean your room.

I like pizza although it is fattening.

Since you are late, we will all be late.

Satinder bought a car because she saved her money.

**Exercise 1:** Underline the conjunctions in the following sentences.

1. Tom likes Linda, but she doesn't like him.

2. I will buy chips or salad.

3. My car won't run, so I have to use my mom's car.

4. I will go if my mother gives me permission.

5. I couldn't leave until my brother got home.

6. I'll call José after I eat.

7. I'm going to do my chores, watch television, and eat a banana.

8. *The Simpsons* isn't on since the basketball game went into overtime.

9. Tom's going with us although he doesn't want to go.

10. Mom made me a cake because she's swell.

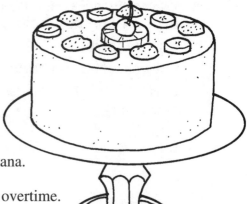

---

　　　　38

# Conjunction Practice

**Exercise 2:** Fill in the blanks with conjunctions.

1. I would like a slice of cheesecake with cherries _____ strawberries.

2. We can go to the movies _____ go to the park.

3. I like Polly _____ she's nice.

4. I will make dinner _____ I finish my homework.

5. _____ you like chocolate, you will like these cookies.

6. Serena wrote me a letter, _____ I haven't seen it.

7. I like Mexican food, _____ I don't like beans.

8. I will give you my book _____ you keep asking for it.

9. This car has power steering _____ air conditioning.

10. You can go, _____ the girls can't go.

11. The teacher will take down your name _____ give you detention.

12. The best choices would be Anthony, Ricky, _____ Danny.

13. Rusty sent me a card, _____ it was nice.

14. Louise is nice, _____ she is also moody.

15. I need some milk, _____ I'm going to the store.

# Introduction to Interjections

| **INTERJECTIONS—Words that show strong or sudden emotion** |
|---|

This is the easiest part of speech. Interjections are the kinds of words or phrases you say when you do something like stub your toe or win a big game. An interjection is often followed by an exclamation point.

Ouch!

Wow!

Ah!

Yay!

Goody, goody gumdrops!

Interjections are not directed at anyone in particular—they are just our way of letting out big feelings.

Gee! Interjections are swell!

**Exercise 1:** Underline the interjections in the following sentences.

1. Jumping Jiminy! This is tasty spinach!

2. Great oogly moogly! I did the wrong math exercises.

3. Yes! We won!

4. Aw, shucks, my pet tarantula died.

5. Goody! You brought candy!

**Exercise 2:** Oh, boy! You get to make up your own interjections! Write five sentences containing interjections. Underline the interjections. Be creative!

_____

_____

_____

_____

_____

# Interjection Practice

**Exercise 3:** Fill in the blanks with interjections.

1. _____! We made it to the finals!

2. _____! I get to go to the party!

3. _____, Suzy got an A!

4. _____! This isn't fair!

5. _____! I can't find my jacks!

6. _____! That hurt!

7. _____, my favorite TV show was canceled!

8. _____! The Rams lost!

9. _____, this is pretty boring!

10. _____, Marsha broke her nose!

11. _____! This is the coolest hair color I've ever had!

12. _____! My mom won't let me keep it!

13. _____! I finally figured out this math problem!

14. _____, all my homework is finished!

15. _____! We're having meatloaf for dinner!

# Parts of Speech Review

**Name**_____

**Exercise 1:** Define the parts of speech.

1. noun: _____

2. pronoun: _____

3. verb: _____

4. adjective: _____

5. adverb: _____

6. preposition: _____

7. conjunction: _____

8. interjection: _____

**Exercise 2:** In the space provided on the following page, identify the part of speech of each underlined word. Match each word to its corresponding number.

      1.                2.  3.  4.       5.    6.  7.    8.
<u>Students</u> should always <u>study</u> <u>hard</u> <u>for</u> grammar <u>tests</u>. <u>They</u> <u>are</u> <u>important</u>.

      9.      10.  11. 12.     13.  14.
Go <u>to</u> the <u>store</u>, <u>and</u> <u>get</u> some <u>lowfat</u> <u>milk</u>, please.

   15.      16.        17.   18.
<u>Oh</u>! I <u>always</u> have to <u>go</u>! I <u>want</u> to watch television.

   19. 20.    21.    22.
<u>Argus</u> <u>is</u> the <u>cutest</u> cat <u>in</u> the world.

     23.       24.   25.  26. 27.      28.
You <u>boys</u> have <u>played</u> <u>extremely</u> <u>well</u>, <u>and</u> I am proud <u>of</u> you.

  29.   30.
<u>Wow</u>! <u>We</u> won!

**Exercise 2:** (cont):

1. _____
2. _____
3. _____
4. _____
5. _____
6. _____
7. _____
8. _____
9. _____
10. _____

11. _____
12. _____
13. _____
14. _____
15. _____
16. _____
17. _____
18. _____
19. _____
20. _____

21. _____
22. _____
23. _____
24. _____
25. _____
26. _____
27. _____
28. _____
29. _____
30. _____

**Exercise 3:** Rewrite each sentence, adding an adjective and an adverb to each. Label the adverb (adv) and the adjective (adj).

1. The girls yelled. _____

2. My mother stood. _____

3. Jose dropped the ball. _____

**Exercise 4:** Rewrite each sentence, adding a prepositional phrase to each. Label the preposition (P) and the object of the preposition (OP).

1. We read the book. _____

2. Argus ate dinner. _____

3. Karla watched TV. _____

**Exercise 5:** Label the underlined verbs as action (A) or linking (L).

1. The cake <u>smells</u> yummy. _____

2. The guests <u>smelled</u> the cat litter. _____

3. I <u>like</u> you. _____

4. You <u>seem</u> upset. _____

5. We <u>felt</u> sick. _____

6. I <u>think</u> about you every day. _____

# Usage Review

Mark **A** if the underlined word is used correctly. Mark **B** if the underlined word is used incorrectly.

_____ 1. Mom and <u>dad</u> are coming to the house.

_____ 2. My <u>doctor</u> said I could not eat this.

_____ 3. I like this <u>fall</u> weather.

_____ 4. I come from the <u>south</u>.

_____ 5. My favorite classes are math and <u>spanish</u>.

_____ 6. The <u>childrens'</u> room is filthy.

_____ 7. I have five <u>daughter's</u>.

_____ 8. This is <u>Jerry's</u> guitar.

_____ 9. That is the <u>teachers'</u> lounge.

_____ 10. Everybody brought <u>their</u> money.

_____ 11. Will someone loan me <u>his or her</u> pencil?

_____ 12. Anyone who lost a book should raise <u>their</u> hand.

_____ 13. Of the two girls, Tammy is <u>shortest</u>.

_____ 14. I am the <u>oldest</u> one in the class.

_____ 15. I feel <u>badly</u>.

_____ 16. That's a <u>real</u> nice sweater.

_____ 17. I ate too much, and I don't feel very <u>well</u>.

_____ 18. You paint <u>good.</u>

_____ 19. I write <u>badly</u>.

_____ 20. Is that a <u>real</u> autographed baseball?

# Editing Checklist for Proper Usage

You can use this editing checklist for any piece of writing you complete. Trade papers with your partner. Based on what you've learned in *Using Parts of Speech*, check your partner's paper for the following:

# of Errors

1. Capitalization: Use a red pencil to circle any capitalization errors.

   Be attentive for errors that involve proper nouns. _____

2. Apostrophes: Use a green pencil to circle any apostrophe errors.

   Make sure that the apostrophe is used correctly to signify possession. _____

3. Pronoun Usage: Use an orange pencil to circle any pronoun errors. _____

4. Verb Usage: Use a blue pencil to circle any verb usage errors. _____

5. Modifiers: Use a black pencil to circle any modifier (adjective or adverb) errors. _____

**Editor's Name** _____

**Writer's Name** _____

-------------------------------------------------------------------------

# Editing Checklist for Proper Usage

You can use this editing checklist for any piece of writing you complete. Trade papers with your partner. Based on what you've learned in *Using Parts of Speech*, check your partner's paper for the following:

# of Errors

1. Capitalization: Use a red pencil to circle any capitalization errors.

   Be attentive for errors that involve proper nouns. _____

2. Apostrophes: Use a green pencil to circle any apostrophe errors.

   Make sure that the apostrophe is used correctly to signify possession. _____

3. Pronoun Usage: Use an orange pencil to circle any pronoun errors. _____

4. Verb Usage: Use a blue pencil to circle any verb usage errors. _____

5. Modifiers: Use a black pencil to circle any modifier (adjective or adverb) errors. _____

**Editor's Name** _____

**Writer's Name** _____

# Answer Key

**Page 6 Introduction to Nouns**
Accept appropriate responses.
**Page 7 Noun Practice**
**Exercises 3 & 4:** Accept appropriate responses.
**Exercise 5**
1. N
2. N
3. N
4. -
5. N
6. N
7. N
8. -
9. N
10. N
11. N
12. N
13. N
14. N
15. N
16. N
17. -
18. -
19. N
20. N
**Page 9 Capitalization Practice**
1. B
2. A
3. B
4. A
5. B
6. A
7. B
8. A
9. B
10. B
11. A
12. B
13. A
14. B
15. A
**Page 10 More Capitalization Practice**
1. B
2. B
3. B
4. A
5. B

6. A
7. B
8. B
9. B
10. B
11. B
12. A
13. B
14. A
15. A
16. A
17. B
18. B
19. B
20. B
**Page 12 Possessives Practice**
**Exercise 1**
1. teachers'
2. country's
3. children's
4. Ross' or Ross's
5. men's
6. cities'
7. dogs'
8. Argus' or Argus's
9. Karla's
10. girls'
**Exercise 2**
1. A
2. B
3. B
4. A
5. B
6. A
7. A
8. B
9. A
10. A
**Page 13 Introduction to Pronouns**
**Exercise 1**
1. her
2. their
3. I, it
4. We
5. you, us
6. That
7. This, my
8. I, she

9. her
10. That, I, it
**Exercise 2:** Accept appropriate responses.
**Page 15 Pronoun-Antecedent Agreement Practice**
1. his or her
2. their
3. her
4. her
5. his or her
6. his
7. their
8. his or her
9. their
10. his
11. his or her
12. his or her
13. their
14. her
15. his or her
**Page 16 Subject and Object Pronouns**
1. I
2. me
3. We
4. she
5. he
6. them
7. they
8. her, us
9. us
10. me
**Page 17 More Subject and Object Pronoun Practice**
1. We
2. us
3. I
4. him, her
5. we
6. me
7. him, me
8. us
9. me
10. him, her
11. her
12. He, I
13. her, him

14. He
15. They
16. I
17. We, they
18. him, her
19. her
20. them, us

## Page 19 Verb Practice
### Exercise 1
1. talks
2. is
3. ran
4. read
5. enjoyed
6. think
7. hope, get
8. like
9. had
10. was

### Exercise 2
1. plays (A)
2. watches (A)
3. likes (A)
4. looks (L)
5. spit (A)
6. is (L)
7. seems (L)
8. looked (A)
9. saw (A)
10. is (L)
11. asked (A)
12. heard (A)
13. sounded (L)
14. is (L)
15. like (A)

## Page 20 More Verb Practice
### Exercise 3
1. ran
2. coughed
3. rode
4. throw
5. will ring
6. ate
7. bought
8. do write
9. will borrow
10. did see

**Exercise 4:** Accept appropriate responses.

## Page 23 Verb Form Practice
1. known, frozen
2. chosen, began
3. worn, stolen
4. chosen, torn
5. rung, have
6. stolen, known
7. have, sung
8. driven, begun
9. began, chosen
10. fell, frozen
11. worn, rung
12. fallen, broken
13. sang, chosen
14. brought, stolen
15. rang, began

## Page 24 Introduction to Adverbs
1. big truck, little car
2. good book
3. cute kitty, sweet face
4. nice (Ms. Bronowski)
5. delicious cake
6. silly thing
7. chocolate ice cream
8. red car, blue one
9. old book
10. shiny, new penny

## Page 25 Adjective Practice
### Exercise 1
1. red car, flat tire
2. early bird
3. empty shed
4. old car, new brakes
5. hot, peppery sauce
6. fat, laughing clown
7. Black soot
8. Dutch windmill, screechy sound
9. young otter, small pond
10. dynamic speaker, large crowd

**Exercise 2:** Accept appropriate responses.

## Page 27 Adjective Degree Practice
1. worst
2. best
3. better

4. worse
5. smartest
6. shorter
7. most exciting
8. younger
9. more careful
10. hairiest
11. better
12. smarter
13. higher
14. highest
15. sillier

## Page 29 Adverb Practice
**Exercise 1:** Accept appropriate responses.

**Exercise 2:** Accept appropriate responses.

## Page 30 More Adverb Practice
Accept appropriate responses.

## Page 31 Modifier Practice
### Exercise 1

1. That's a *very nice* car you have.

2. She writes *pretty well*.

3. Dina sings *really badly*.

4. This paper is *barely readable*.

5. Karla *really* likes *crispy* cookies.

# Answer Key (cont.)

**Page 33 Adjectives vs. Adverbs Practice**

1. good
2. well
3. good
4. well
5. well
6. bad
7. badly
8. bad
9. bad
10. badly
11. real
12. really
13. really
14. really
15. really
16. well
17. well
18. bad
19. bad
20. really

**Page 35 Preposition Practice**
**Exercise 1**

1. <u>at</u> the (South Pole)
2. <u>during</u> the (speech)
3. <u>with</u> the (bathwater)
4. <u>in</u> the (pan)
5. <u>on</u> (TV)
6. <u>under</u> the (table)
7. <u>to</u> the (movies)
8. <u>across</u> the (road)
9. <u>on</u> the (table)
10. <u>to</u> the (top)

**Exercise 2:** Accept appropriate responses.

**Page 36 More Preposition Practice**
Accept appropriate responses.

**Page 38 Introduction to Conjunctions**

1. but
2. or
3. so
4. if
5. until
6. after
7. and
8. since
9. although
10. because

**Page 39 More Conjunction Practice**
Accept appropriate responses.

**Page 40 Introduction to Interjections**
**Exercise 1**

1. Jumping Jiminy!
2. Great oogly moogly!
3. Yes!
4. Aw shucks
5. Goody!

**Exercise 2:** Accept appropriate responses.

**Page 41 More Interjection Practice**
Accept appropriate responses.

**Pages 42–43 Parts of Speech Review**
**Exercise 1**

1. noun—names a person, place, thing, or idea
2. pronoun—replaces a noun
3. verb—shows action or state of being
4. adjective—describes nouns, pronouns
5. adverb—describes verbs, adjectives, adverbs
6. preposition—shows relationship between other words
7. conjunction—joins or connects other words
8. interjection—shows sudden or strong emotion

**Exercise 2**

1. noun
2. verb
3. adverb
4. preposition
5. noun
6. pronoun
7. verb
8. adjective
9. preposition
10. noun
11. conjunction
12. verb
13. adjective
14. noun
15. interjection
16. adverb
17. verb
18. verb
19. noun
20. verb
21. adjective
22. preposition
23. noun
24. verb
25. adverb
26. adverb
27. conjunction
28. preposition
29. interjection
30. pronoun

**Exercise 3**
Accept appropriate responses.
**Exercise 4**
Accept appropriate responses.
**Exercise 5**

1. L
2. A
3. A
4. L
5. L
6. A

**Page 44 Usage Review**

1. B
2. A
3. A
4. B
5. B
6. B
7. B
8. A
9. A
10. B
11. A
12. B
13. B
14. A
15. B
16. B
17. A
18. B
19. A
20. A